HOW THEN SHALL I LIVE

HOW THEN
SHALL I LIVE

✒

ONENESS REVEALED

by Michele Longo O'Donnell

La Vida Press
Boerne, Texas

Library of Congress Cataloging
in Publication Data

ISBN 1523495308   softcover

Published in 2016
La Vida Press
107 Scenic Loop Road
Boerne, Texas 78006
830-755-8767

Living Beyond Disease
www.livingbeyonddisease.com

———   ———

TABLE OF CONTENTS

DEDICATION

I walked into the room where lay a small child, her eyes wide with fear, emaciated, dying... with the surrounding belief of those with her, caring for her...indeed the whole earth as well...believing in the power of an evil imagination (disease) capable of destroying her life. No one knowing that her life is the One Life, incapable of destruction. No one knowing who she is.

> Dear God, Let there be Light, understanding, truth to rise up and swallow up the insanity we have accepted as "real," as "needed," as "legitimate." Awaken us to know that you have surrounded us with every wonderful thing we need for a lifetime of peace, of joy, of abundant goodness.
>
> May our eyes be opened to see it all around us. To enter into it.

ACKNOWLEDGEMENTS

I am grateful beyond words to the Spirit of God who gives me understanding and the words to speak and to write. I am grateful for our high calling and God's intention and purpose for each one of us...as One.

Thank you to Melissa, my faithful and long-time friend, for the editing. Thank you to Lee, who meticulously searches out the many scripture references for the readers to further their studies. Thank you to Kay, my wonderful assistant, and again to Melissa, for their constant encouragement. Special thanks to Melissa who needed to leave her clinic patients to run down the hall many, many times a day to fix this computer. It has had a mind of its own throughout!

INTRODUCTION

Beyond the realm of "doing" to achieve a spiritual end...
Beyond the realm of thinking about truth, speaking truth...
Beyond the realm of overcoming some form of darkness...
Beyond using one power to overcome another power...
Using Light to overcome darkness...
Is a state of Light, silent, swirling Light, vibrating to the
frequency of its own Being.

Swirling about...not doing anything, but simply Being.
Full of its own majesty, its own radiance, its own blazing
glory...
It fills all space and we are in it...one with it.
It is who we are, who we have always been.

Now we realize ourselves as that Light Being.
Filling the vastness of its own realm is Spirit. The sum total
of all that is. The most Holy Spirit, the fullness of God in
expression. This activity of Spirit, this expression in and

through us is grace. It is purposeful, with focus and intention.

We cannot enter into this moment, this space, carrying words or thought, weights or concerns. We become still, quiet, gazing at the swirling, blazing Light. Feeling its holiness, we become its holiness.

Without effort we are One.

CHAPTER ONE

FOUNDATIONAL TRUTHS

"What is man that thou art mindful of him? Or the son of man that thou visited him?"[1]

Why are we here?

Who are we?

Where have we come from?

What is our responsibility here?

How is this to be done?

Immediately we are faced with two drastically conflicting ideologies. Which one we choose will determine the landscape of our lives. One is the voice of religion throughout the generations. I call it the John the Baptist realm of thought. It starts out declaring our present failure as a mortal and the things required of us to gain what we need to "please God" and ultimately secure eternal life. John is this voice who declares that to qualify for this we must "bring forth fruits worthy of repentance,"[2] cleanse ourselves of internal transgressions and live a life of purity and goodness. But he stops there. Since mankind has done this forever and still we seem to be spinning our wheels in the sand, there must be more. And there is. Now enters Jesus who does not negate what John has said but takes us to another atmosphere of thought entirely. Remaining in the John the Baptist thought leaves us totally absorbed in our own existence. Our focus is on how we are doing to meet this standard or how we are failing. We never feel entirely worthy and indeed we can't, because the whole scenario depends on us and we are never sure. When faced with challenges we immediately go to "what did I do wrong?" Or "what didn't I do that I should have done?" We are unable to gain the necessary "conscience void of offense both toward God and man."[3] We are continually reminded of how unworthy we are and will always be. This is the reason for human suffering. Somehow (and we usually don't know how) we deserved it, needed it, just because we are alive! This is the conclusion of the entire Old Testament or Covenant. The bottom line is, "If you do it right, you will be blessed but if you do it wrong you will be cursed." No one being entirely sure of what the "it" really is.

The huge lesson to be learned is that mankind cannot "do it" and needs to stop trying. The book of Hebrews, chapter 4, tells us to "enter into the rest of God" and let him do whatever needs to be done. Hebrews, chapters 9 and 10, boldly declares the utter end of the old in favor of the new. This ends mankind's efforts and subsequent failures. This places the whole scenario in the lap of the Almighty where it belongs and this is called grace.

So Jesus came along to teach us about this living grace

and how it plays out. To gain this understanding, one idea needs to end to make room for the new to appear. Hence, John the Baptist lost his head in favor of a new head or thought. Now an entirely new idea came to be. A new way to think, to live, and with new experiences and a new hope. Jesus was all about ushering in a world dominated by the grace and glory of the kingdom of God. "As in Heaven, so on earth."[4] "A new heaven and a new earth."[5] One of peace, where the "lion (human nature) lays down with the Lamb (divine nature)."[6] One devoid of pain, suffering, disease, and death. Isaiah, chapter 25, tells us, "He will destroy the veil cast over all people and the covering over all nations." (By doing this) he will swallow up death and will wipe away tears from off all faces (eliminating all sorrow, pain, suffering, disease). The veil is the Old Testament mentality about the nature of God, with all its laws and impossible-to-maintain righteousness. Grace is the end of man's failure and the beginning of a world that IS the Garden of God, Paradise. A New Heaven and a New Earth. Right here. Right now.

Where the Old Testament taught us of a god of wrath and harsh judgment, the New Testament teaches us of a God who is Love, Mercy and whose grace actually sends the Holy Spirit into our hearts to do for us what needs to be done. This takes the burden to be righteous off of us and places it in the only place that it can be fulfilled. All we need to do is yield and follow. "For this is the covenant I make with my people; I will put my laws into their mind and write them in their hearts; and I will be to them a God and they shall be to me a people. And they shall not teach every man his neighbor saying know the Lord, for all shall know me from the least to the greatest. For I will forgive their iniquity and remember their sin no more."[7]

Jesus came not so much to prove what he could do as to prove what we could do and how to achieve it. He did this not by what he did BUT BY WHAT HE KNEW. So a radical correction in thought must enter in, which will produce a radical correction in our entire experience. We must go back to the beginning...for an error in premise will of necessity produce an error in conclusion.

The blind religious thought fights for its right to live. It argues for suffering to be legitimate and needful while all the while it runs to and fro to find an escape from it all. It argues for morality to be the issue, seeing itself as "moral" and therefore in good standing with God. And all the while it separates itself from others who it deems polluted, ignoring Love and acceptance and grace. Love actually being the "fulfillment of the whole law!"[8]

As it was in Jesus' day so it remains.

So returning to our basic questions in the beginning of this chapter...

The significant importance of the answers to these questions came from Jesus himself when the ever-challenging religious leaders of his day asked him where he received his authority and ability to do the astonishing things that he did. He replied that if they knew the answers to these questions, as he did, they too could do as he did.

So let's start with who we are and where we have come from. The answer to these two questions will determine what level of consciousness we will choose to live from, the imprisoning mortal or the liberating Divine.

If we choose, as the whole world has, that we started as a seed, with a specific DNA code and a genetic blueprint, we have chosen the very limited human experience called mortality. This consigns us to all the pain, suffering, diseases, and ultimate death that we see all around us. This is entirely governed by the law of chance. The dice rolls and we jump through whatever hoop appears. Sometimes good, oftentimes very evil and threatening. If good, we never know how long it will last. Not often a very secure feeling. If bad, how long will it last? What must I do? Will I survive it? And then what? Where do I go from here?

But if we choose to know that "it is He who has made us and not we ourselves,"[9] that we comprise a "DNA" of only DIVINE NATURE, that we bear the likeness of our Source (each seed reproduces after its own kind)[10] and that NO MATTER WHAT appears or happens that denies this...THAT is an immutable fact of being, for He is immutable. We have then chosen the Divine consciousness, or the identity of the immortal. ("This mortal MUST put on immortality.")[11] If we choose to know that "we have been IN HIM since before the foundation of the world,"[12] and that "he has been our dwelling place since before the mountains were brought forth and before the earth and the worlds were formed"[13]...and that "we were there before the world was formed as the sons of God shouting for joy before his greatness and glory" (Job, chapter 38:7)...then we can lay claim to our eternal divine nature and all the security and wonders of it all. Ezekiel, chapter 44, tells us that we "possess Him as He possesses us."

What all this is saying is that we are now, and have always been what we have been scrambling for, suffering for and aching to reach for generations. Moreover, we were not so much born as sent from a realm of existence we enjoyed from forever. Just as Jesus declares throughout the book of John, "For this cause have I been sent!" But he didn't stop there! No, there was one more critical thing he knew. He knew that he brought all the power, goodness, grace and perfection of heaven with him when he came. He knew he was sent for a mission and that he was fully equipped to do whatever he faced successfully because he carried all the attributes and characteristics of his Divine Source with him. "Let this very mind be in you which was in Christ Jesus!"[14]

Unlike the Old Testament religion that challenged and finally murdered him, he was not needing to gain something he didn't have, but only to learn to use what he possessed in order to fulfill his Father's Divine purpose for him. And so it is with us.

Jesus did lay hold of these facts and this elevated his capacity to know that nothing would be impossible to him. This understanding fully embraced, would give him a perpetual state of certainty and dominion over all the madness of mortal thinking. He did not relate to being "born here" but to being "sent" here from an eternal state of being...for an eternal purpose. And when that was fulfilled, he then would return to his eternal state of being. Again and again "let this mind be also in you."

This was his answer to those who asked from where he received his authority. They never heard it though, just as they don't hear it now. He of course was speaking to those who "have ears to hear"[15] about themselves as well. An understanding we must embrace to if we are to fulfill the command to "take dominion and subdue"[15] the erroneous thinking and subsequent chaos of the world.

Which leads us to why we are here. Certainly not to gain anything that we do not possess already (for the kingdom of Heaven is within you).[17] Certainly not to pay for sins we never committed, or sins someone else committed. Certainly not for any of the endless myopic reasons given to us by those who clearly have no idea themselves. All of which causes us to keep our attention squarely upon ourselves and away from our mission. ("Take no thought for your life.")[18] This is NOT ABOUT US trying to gain righteousness and heaven. This is about exactly what it says, taking dominion and subduing all the works (thoughts, ideas) of darkness and chaos and confusion resulting in the convoluted human living we see. This is the Kingdom of Heaven. Jesus came to cause us to experience life "ON Earth as it is in heaven."[19]

A critical thought which must be challenged is the widespread belief that although we may have come from the perfection of Paradise, we somehow left it behind and now must scramble to regain what we lost. But we were sent to take dominion and subdue and we are well able to do this because we yet contain all of the divine nature, which of course is already in a state of perpetual dominion over all darkness.

So we start experience by experience, situation by situation, challenge by challenge...all the while knowing then that "for this cause have we too have been sent."[20] To use every adversity that presents itself to us, or to humanity in general, to overcome and prove the kingdom of heaven is here now and fully operational. Contrary to what we have forever been told...we do not experience adversity because we deserve it, earned it, need it or the like. We are sent to it to establish the dominion of light over darkness, order over chaos, love over fear, life over death. It's not about you! It's always about something so much higher than you or me. It's about the honor and glory of the kingdom of God. On earth as it is in heaven.

I call this an opportunity to "turn it around." Every time a challenge appears, instead of immediately thinking it is against me personally, (thus racing around trying to figure out what to do), I remember who I am and why I am and know that this is not about me...but it is a challenge to the Ever Present, Omnipotent and Immutable God...not me at all. This will immediately engage the grace of the eternal Presence to subdue and quash the words and works of the proud and boastful evil one.

We are here as a conduit to the grace (activity) of God as he reveals himself and his governing authority to a world crying and travailing in pain and confusion waiting for the "manifestation of the sons of God."[21]

And this will appear and we will grow and gain in a greater understanding of the truths of both God and man.

CHAPTER TWO

HOW IS THIS TO BE ACCOMPLISHED?

Again we must look at the life and words of Jesus, who was so successful at this. There was nothing, no matter how horrible the picture, no matter how threatening the belief about it, that he could not correct...bringing the Kingdom of God to light for all to see and hopefully believe. He never measured the intensity of any appearance of darkness or the significance of it, to ascertain if he could correct it...for he knew that no matter how insistent the adversary boasted of its power and ability to destroy, there was only One Power in heaven and earth. And the fullness of that was within him.

He said, "All power in heaven and earth is mine."[1] Then he declared we too possess all the power in heaven and earth, for we have come from the same Source, carrying the same nature and to fulfill the same purpose. "Go ye therefore and do as I have done,"[2] (for you also possess all power in heaven and earth.)

First of all he never doubted where he came from, the

true nature and substance of who he was, nor what he was sent to do. This is clearly the first and most significant foundation of consciousness of anyone desiring to fulfill their reason for coming here.

He never succumbed to the hysterical madness of religion which consigns mankind to defeat and failure before he ever starts! Then builds an empire of erroneous thoughts and doctrines around such falsehood, acquiescing to all manner of pain and suffering, and declaring mankind deserving of it and needing it as well. But the most evil and insidious doctrine of them all is that they attribute this to God, himself. And call it love! No small wonder Jesus said of them, "You make the truth of God of none effect by your traditions (of thought) and doctrines. You are the blind leading the blind.[3] And that you keep men from entering into their God given inheritance of the kingdom of heaven and fail to enter in yourselves!"[4] Lord! It's time we turned from such death producing thought and begin to derive our understanding from the same Source that Jesus used for his success and understanding.

He chose to see only what God sees and knows. Man sees as he has been taught. Man sees according to his fears and beliefs. God sees according to what he knows is the eternal, immutable truth of man, made in the beauty, order and perfection of his Creator.

If he did not see mankind and all of life as it presently appears...how did he see it? He saw it in its unbroken and exalted state as it was formed by One who is entirely exalted, whole, complete and immutable. It was this KNOWING that made the corrections that we have come to call

miracles. It will be our coming into this same consciousness which will enable us to do the same.

In every correction of error (healing) that we witness
or read about, someone saw beyond what the masses
saw...knew something beyond what the masses knew, and
this seeing, knowing, was the power of God to correct the
whole consciousness of man, causing him to see and experience what never changes. Namely the beauty and order of the Kingdom of God, here and now. Ecclesiastes,
chapter 3:14, says, "Whatsoever God has made shall be
forever. Nothing can be added to it nor can anything be
taken from it." Creation remains forever in the eternal
state it was formed in from the perfect Mind of God. No
human fear, belief or doctrine can ever change that. It remains for us to take hold of this that we also might "do
the works of him who sent us."[5]

You might have found this in one if my previous books,
but I want to share with you an experience I had over forty
years ago in response to this very question.

I had a clear advantage in that I was not indoctrinated
into any particular religious thought as a child. To be sure
I "picked up" the general idea that God was responsible
for all the sufferings of the world, and that he created something incredibly evil and set it loose on us because we were
such miserable sinners. (One wonders how pure goodness
and perfection can spawn evil in the first place, or anything that becomes evil, for that matter.) But after my first
all-consuming experience with Jesus I began to doubt what
was commonly accepted and I asked a million
questions...but I asked my questions of the only Source

that I dared to believe. I read where Jesus sent us the Spirit of Truth that "would lead and guide us into all truth" and would "bring to our remembrance all that he has spoken to us."[6] I believed these words and so consequently he was immediately my only source of understanding.

One of my most frequently asked questions was, "How did Jesus heal?" I read that we were sent to do the same but I never understood how that was to be done. It was imperative to me that I find out.

One day while I was having an appointment with a patient, a very unexpected thing arrested my attention. I heard this question, "How do you suppose Jesus healed the man with the withered hand?" This was referring to a story in Luke, Chapter 6, of a man appearing in the synagogue with a deformed hand and Jesus healed it. My immediate response was "I have no idea how he did any of the healings he did!" The answer was immediate and life changing. "He never saw it withered."

Then what did he see? It was to be several years later before I would come to that understanding. Of course he saw what others saw...but with his heart he saw something so much clearer, so much more truthful, so much more eternal. He saw what Perfection created. And that could only be perfection. And with that clear awareness foremost in his heart and mind, the picture presented changed radically.

Now, did the hand change? Or did the 'mind that observed' behold something different because of what it knew was true? The answer is the mind that observed caused the correction in the picture. Or better put, the consciousness which observed caused what it knew to appear.

Many years later I had the privilege of watching this process first hand. I was presiding over one of our annual Living Beyond Disease retreats to a group of about 120 folks. Many of whom I had never met. The last day of the retreat we had our usual question and answer time. But this one was different because instead of it taking that direction the folks began to stand up and relate spontaneous healings they had received over the weekend. One such young lady said she was healed of breast cancer and sat right back down again. I noticed that her mother and her sister looked at her in confusion, but we moved on. A few days later I received a call from her. She told me that three years ago one of her breasts had been removed due to breast cancer but that two weeks before the retreat, on one of her every six month checks, she was told that her x-rays showed massive spreading throughout her entire thorax. She was shown the films and told to restart chemotherapy again. But she declined. She told them she was going to a retreat in two weeks and would see them after. Her mother nor her sister were aware of this reoccurrence.

Now she was at the point of needing to hand-carry the films from her primary care to her oncologist. She found herself full of fear of what he would say. She said she knew she received a healing at the retreat but was now filled with fear again. I told her that I would pray. And I did.

About three days later she remembered to call me back and she was squealing like my granddaughter often does. She said he put the films up on the viewing screen and everything looked normal! With that he told her she looked great and not to come back for at least a year.

Now the films didn't change. They don't have life. They don't have a consciousness. No! The consciousness which viewed them changed.

So then it was not what Jesus DID that caused the healings, but what he KNEW that caused the healings.

Logically we can know that Good can only bring forth good. That the Pure and perfect One can only reproduce purity and perfection. That what comes forth from the altogether Unchangeable One must of necessity also be immutable and never subject to change no matter what is believed.

But how do we get from the logical conclusions of the eternal truth to the corrections of the material/mortal conditions?

More clearly stated...how do we observe something different even knowing the truth? Here is where folks go off the track. Just hearing and believing with the mind can never bring forth the desired results.

John declares to us that the Spirit and the Truth must agree.[7] We have the truth. What we need is a correction in our spirit or consciousness. Many I have witnessed believe that by constant repetition of the truth, it must appear. If they say it enough it will make the change needed in consciousness. They are sadly disappointed.

Truth which is known only in the mind is incapable of changing anything, even though it is a necessary stepping stone towards the change in consciousness. The truth must be accompanied by an experience with the truth giver...and this is accomplished not by mortal man but by the Holy Spirit alone.

In frustration many change the truth of the nature and person of God to fit the human picture. But we must never change the truth of God into a lie. We must find the way to hold to the truth and let the Spirit, the absolute ONLY power, to flow through the mind, into the consciousness, thereby correcting, healing and making all things appear as new. So it is not in man himself to make this correction but it is entirely the presence and working of the Spirit of Truth to bring this forth. Again the Spirit and the truth must agree.

And with that chiasm in front of us at every turn, how do we proceed? Thank God that what is impossible for the mortal is quite natural with the Immortal One.

We've spoken of the absolute truth of God, of our purpose in the realization and experience of this throughout the earth and the subsequent appearance of the kingdom of peace and perfection. We know from the failure of the "Old" Testament, (read Hebrews 9,10) where mankind attempted to bring forth righteousness and perfection by his many efforts and failed...the need for a new, more perfect way, one where God alone would do what only God can do. And this is accomplished by the Presence, the power and the workings of the Spirit of God alone. This is living by grace. Grace is by definition the activity of the Spirit in the lives of man, doing for man what man is incapable of doing for himself.

Einstein's famous quote fits here. "No problem can be solved by the same consciousness that created it."

Since this is our hope and indeed the hope of the world,

we will look at the Spirit of God and examine its many facets and workings. We will come to understand it in a much more intimate way and therefore learn the value of complete dependence upon it.

WHAT IS CONSCIOUSNESS?

Let me digress a minute here and define what consciousness really is before we go on.

What is consciousness?

Is it something we think? Something we believe?

No. Consciousness is not the mind. That's why you cannot change or correct it by using the mind, human effort, willing it, praying, repeating truths or scriptures.

It is much deeper than the mind. It is a "sense" or a vague, but very real awareness of something. Something we all act out from but few know why we act or react as we do. We unknowingly draw into our consciousness from a realm or atmosphere of thought that surrounds us. We attract to ourselves for good or bad depending upon what we hold in consciousness.

Why do some folks just make money without effort while others remain in poverty for a lifetime? Why do some folks never get sick while others go from one physical problem to another as long as they live? Why do some folks have happy, fulfilling relationships that last a lifetime while others sink into a lifetime of loneliness? Why do some succeed at everything they do while others fail at every turn...or just don't even try at all? Why do some see only the good and expect it to appear while others live out from a critical, condemning nature, seeing conflict and drama everywhere they look? Why do some struggle all their lives and never really amount to anything? Never get ahead? Always in the red? Their dreams never fulfilled. Why do some see an enemy around every corner? Always reacting? Always ducking? The answer is what is being held in consciousness.

Some people call this the soul. It might be just that. I do know that the soul is of a feminine gender, unlike the spirit which is a strong masculine gender. The soul will attract and take into itself whatever is dominate in the atmosphere. Until something stronger begins to occupying that space.

So how do we experience a correction of the consciousness? By something stronger appearing within consciousness. Something more truthful. Something eternal, permanent.

Not by the mind. Not by the will. But solely by the function of the Holy Spirit.

King David wished to build a house for the Lord. He was deeply humbled that God did so much for him and he desired to do something for God. (Read 1 Chronicles 22.) But he was engaged in wars and much conflict while establishing Jerusalem, and the house could only be built in quietness and peace. So the building of the house fell upon his son Solomon, for he reigned during a time of peace and prosperity. Now God said of the house that he would place his name there and that he would dwell there forever. We must understand that the house is the individual consciousness of man, who under the direction of the Holy Spirit is built to actually house the "Name" or nature/attributes of God...until our conscious awareness is altogether the mind and heart of God. "And of his fullness have we all received."[1] It is in this way only that we can attain to the state of "Oneness" that Jesus spoke of in chapter 17 of the book of John. Only then can we "know" him as we are known of him.[2]

We must, and will, all come to the place where we "cease from our own works"[3]...lay down all of our own efforts to achieve and succeed spiritually, and "enter into the rest,"[4] or peace of a life lived out from grace...the workings of the Holy Spirit. In the Old Testament book of Isaiah, chapter 58, beginning with verse 6 clear to the end of the chapter, God is giving us a clear picture of a heart that is prepared to house the fullness of the nature of the eternal God himself. This is the "rest," or Sabbath day consciousness, which is a precursor to establishing "Oneness." This consciousness is entirely directed and built by the Spirit of God.

Just to isolate a portion of this writing, beginning with verses 6-7, "...to loose the bands of wickedness, to undo the heavy burdens, and to let the oppressed go free, and that you break every yoke...to deal thy bread to the hungry, and that thou bring the poor that are cast out to thy house and when you see the naked, that you cover him...and that you hide not yourself from your own flesh..." the last segment actually means that you humbly and deeply examine your own soul.

All that refers to our actions with others, and it is all of a very spiritual nature. But moving down to verse 13 we find a deeper commitment, and that to God, himself. "...that you cease from doing your own pleasure, (in favor of doing only the will of God)...not going your own way, nor finding your own pleasures...not even speaking your own words."

All that we experience in this lifetime, if we surrender our steps to him who has called us, is aiming us toward hearts or consciousness' reflective of the heart of God and thus prepared to be the home of the fullness of God.

So I believe the answer is found in the Name of God. The name, once again, refers to the nature, the characteristics, the being of God. By whatever name you call God...God dwells in an atmosphere of pure consciousness. God IS pure consciousness. This atmosphere knows no evil because it attracts no evil. It lives and emanates only that which is pure, rich in beauty, full of harmony, encompassing all, pouring out from its storehouse of goodness, always giving the increase. Full of knowledge and wisdom and understanding. It sees only itself and knows only out from its purity. When this is experienced by any one of us...when any attribute of God is actually known or felt in our hearts...this then displaces whatever mortal awareness we previously held. The stronger displaces the weaker. This is God, by his Spirit building his house, the

New Jerusalem, the City of God.

To correct an error in consciousness:

How do you know if you are carrying one? By that which appears.

It cannot be changed! It must be replaced! No amount of psychology, counselling, self-help, or drugs can correct it. It must be replaced with something else. Anyone can change the outward behavior but the consciousness is another realm altogether.

Again, the human consciousness is formed by the atmosphere of thought surrounding us. Some factors that negatively form our consciousness might be; Children in war zones. Children orphaned. Children abused. Children raised under a fearful mother, a bullying father. Taking care of someone sick and finding yourself holding a fear of that sickness. Surrounded by hate, anger. Watching movies or television stories of conflict, violence, deception and the like. Many such influences place a sense of something, introduce something impure into the soul or consciousness. All around us is the covering of the chaos and confusion of mass human consciousness. The only solution is to place yourself under the covering of the Holy Spirit and grace. The stronger displacing the weaker.

But the name of God is constant. It is not influenced by anything other than its own nature, its own "knowing". It definitely is not reactive to anything that might appear out from this insane, convoluted atmosphere of consciousness called mortality. It doesn't get mad, doesn't punish, doesn't threaten, is not disappointed. It sees through the eyes of pure Love. GOD DOES NOT REACT.

He acts only out from his own nature (Love) because "he cannot deny himself."

As long as you choose to live out from this chaotic atmosphere you come under the law of "sowing and reaping, cause and effect." It is in place to keep us from self-destructing. It offers consequences so we can make better choices.

But God is Mercy. And Mercy is the sweeping away of whatever is influencing your thought, your experiences that are harmful and constricting.

Wisdom is using every adverse situation you find yourself facing, and rather than wiggling and squirming to extricate yourself...instead know that this is an opportunity to cooperate in the building of the Christ consciousness within. For a moment forgetting the problem, leaving it behind, you go to a quiet place in your heart and ask God to reveal to you his name. "What am I missing here? What is it about your pure nature which will dissolve and replace this experience?" When you know it and you begin to feel the Presence of it, you have just witnessed the Holy Spirit displacing whatever thought or attitude that lent itself to this situation and you are free. But the greatest realization of all is that you have just built another portion of the God-awareness within your consciousness. One step closer to a state of Oneness. One step closer to "greater things than this shall you do."[5]

Zechariah, chapter 4 verse 7, declares and instructs us to shout "grace, grace" to every mountain that stand before us, knowing that as we do the activity and Presence of the Holy Spirit will dissolve it before our eyes. We are surrounded on every side by all the heavenly help we will ever need for any and every situation we encounter. Shouldn't we expect that from God who is Faithful and True?

CHAPTER FOUR

INTRODUCTION TO THE HOLY SPIRIT

Often the forgotten aspect of Deity, we fail to realize that Jesus himself said that without the influence of the Spirit he could do none of the works that he did.[1] He said he was a "man under authority,"[2] speaking of the guidance of the Spirit. His entire life was dependent upon this Spirit...as must ours be also.

You might recall that when the Spirit descended upon Jesus at the Jordan River (again signifying a total surrender of self-interests and concerns) it filled him and consecrated him. Meaning it set him aside to fulfill a divine purpose. It also enabled him to not only perform astonishing works, but to speak with wisdom and understanding and authority beyond what was ever before heard.

Biblically, and in most of the earliest cultures recorded, the Spirit is referred to as the wind, the air, the breath. The common prefix here is "pneumo." All referring to the wind, air and breath. The Spirit fills all space and is not only as near as the wind and air...it is the wind and air. It is not only as near to us as our breath...it is our breath. The all-encompassing vastness of it cannot be comprehended by the mind of man. But we know we are surrounded by it. It is the Omni Presence of God in whom "we live, move and have our being."[3]

Since the "mortal consciousness" cannot enter the kingdom of God (John, chapter 3:5-8), it falls upon the Spirit to awaken each soul to the higher consciousness of the Eternal Spirit Man...the Christ.

Once Spirit enters the picture we cease to hold the reins of our lives. "The wind blows where it will and although we hear the sound, we cannot tell where it came from or where it goes...so is everyone that is born of Spirit."[4] (Awakened to a new living perception of life)

Moreover, our purpose for being "sent" here cannot be known or fulfilled except by the workings of this Spirit. (John 3:34)

Spirit is also referred to as water, specifically depicted as a river flowing. Psalms 46 says, "There is a river, the steams thereof make glad the city of God." And we are that city, the place where God has chosen to dwell. The "streams" that flow through us are the many characteristics/the various aspects of the nature of God.

We read in the second chapter of Genesis that out from the garden of God, Paradise, which is at the very core and Source of our being, flows a mighty rushing, gushing river that breaks forth into four rivers. The names of the four rivers are Pison, where gold is found in abundance (spiritually gold refers to obtaining the nature of God). The second is Gihon, the third is Hiddekel and the fourth is the great river Euphrates. All of these names refer to experiencing abundance of all that is needed. For when the Spirit is freely flowing it does indeed contain all that God is and all that creation needs for peace and prosperity and goodness.

Also we find in Ezekiel, chapter 47, a description of a rushing river proceeding forth from the Throne room of God. (Again the soul of man) It is so magnificent in its intrinsic splendor that wherever and whatever the waters touch there is a healing or restitution which takes place. But here there are two significant factors which we do not find spoken of in the previous references to Spirit as a river. One is that it must be flowing to be of any value. Areas not found in the mainstream of the river and where the water is trapped and stagnating is "given over to death." We have learned of "potential energy" and "kinetic energy." Potential is exactly what it says, it has the potential to have life and energy but unless it is flowing, it expresses none. Where kinetic can be as powerful as the dynamics of the flow. Jesus also said that "out of our bellies shall flow rivers of living waters."[5] The river flows in response to our "pouring out" of our lives as we are led of Spirit to do so. The stagnation comes as we begin to become ensnared in self-protection, self-interests (how will this be good for me?) and self-centeredness.

The second point that differs is that it speaks of man standing on the bank of the river and his progressive, albeit hesitant, entrance into the river. Once he gives up fear and the need to control and enters fully in, he is carried forth by the joyful and life-giving waters of God.

For years I enjoyed the idea of being carried by the river, knowing it would always lead me to wonderful experiences and destinations. Because of that I carried a strong sense of confidence and assurance no matter whatever might appear attempting to interfere. In my mind I hugged my children and later my grandchildren close to me within this river so they also might experience safety and prosper in whatever they set themselves to do. When patients seemed to be struggling I held them tight within the peaceful flow of the river.

One night I dreamed (or it actually happened) of what was the great Throne room of God. I was there with all the myriads of angels, the twenty-four elders spoken of in Revelation, chapter 4, and the four "creatures"...all in a place of ecstatic joy and indescribable peace. I was there for what seemed to be a very long time. I never wanted to leave. And the life-giving river was there also, pouring out towards the earth and all its inhabitants. There were trees, grasses, flowers, birds...all of which seemed to be singing, as the sound of musical instruments...and enveloped in Love.

The most significant part of this was that I knew that it was all within ME. I contained the Garden of God. Or I was the Garden of God. I was the result of this place of Paradise. Because it existed, I existed. And I knew I had always been here and forever would be here also.

This was the Eternal Life that I lived before I entered this mortal experience, and to which I would return. The greatest, most arresting thing I was aware of was that I had actually brought it with me. Forever gone was the age old religious doctrine that spoke of my "fall from it," my separation from it, and the never ending struggle to regain it.

I was mostly aware that this river that I had enjoyed being a part of for so many years was actually within me, not something outside of me that I chose to enter or not. Now I knew it was a part of me. A major part of me. And in fact was the "creative energy or principle" that formed me for my years of inhabiting the earth. It was the very substance of my existence. I was not made of flesh and bones but entirely of the energy of this river. It was my life. Not just where I came from but my life. I knew that to utterly know this (feel it, experience it) was all that was needed for any aspect of Life to appear. It was the core of healing for anyone.

I also knew that since I inhabited this Throne room, or Source, I could actually direct the flow of this river (Spirit) wherever I felt the Spirit directing me to do so. And it would fully respond to me every time.

I woke up dizzy from the enormity of this experience and it has remained with me since.

CHAPTER FIVE

GOD IS BUILDING A HOUSE

Remember that the goal or intention of God is to reveal his nature, his person, to and through his creation...specifically man. When this new consciousness is finally realized, all of creation will also enjoy the benefits of the new heaven and the new earth. "All creation groans and travails together in pain waiting for the manifestation of the sons of God."[1] Peace will rule the whole atmosphere of earth. All chaos, confusion, greed and selfishness will be swallowed up by the fullness of Divine Love and pure goodness, which will have filled the hearts of all mankind. And all this is the workings of the Spirit of God within us.

God is surely building a house "eternal in the heavens not made with hands."[2] Not needing or wanting human effort to bring this forth. Only our love and trust.

God said of his house that he would place his name there and it would remain forever. That name would be written in our foreheads, a new name that no one would know except he to whom it was given.[3]

Remember when he breathed his Spirit into the nostrils of Adam (symbolic of all mankind) and man became a living soul? This was the beginning of the building of a new consciousness, for the nostrils and forehead are the same word in the Hebrew language. The forehead is the frontal lobe of the brain which houses the consciousness of the creature.

"A new heart will I give you, a new spirit put within you and I'll take away your stony heart. I will put my spirit in you and you shall be my people and I will be your God."[4] These are in part the words of the New Covenant...the absolute promise of an absolute faithful God.

The entirety of this work...the bringing forth of the "many membered only begotten Son,"[5] is from beginning to end the work of the Spirit in the affairs of men...Grace. Once we cease from our own religious efforts, labors, opinions, judgments, logical conclusions, etc., and we are finally ready to just stop and trust, the Spirit is right there to take over and make all things new. By bringing forth the name of the fullness of God from deep within you. Whatever aspect of that divine nature that is needed for whatever the situation.

Our grossly distorted and total mis-apprehension of the true nature of God is the problem and the revealing of the true, the real and the immutable (unchangeable) name is the answer. Unfortunately (or fortunately) we experience our lives in direct proportion to how we ascertain his nature, his intentions and purposes.

"To know him aright is Life eternal."

"To know him aright is peace forevermore."

"Acquaint thyself with him and be at peace, so shall thy good come unto thee."[6]

"And this is Life eternal, that they might know me and him who sent me."[7]

So the clearer we know, not simply hear, of his true unchangeable nature, the sooner our lives will reflect the fullness of all the goodness that awaits us.

There are many Names, or revelations of God. Throughout our lives we will have the opportunity to experience each one. Again the Wisdom of God is that we use every adverse situation, great or small, to reach out to "know" him. "Here is this situation, Father. Show me what I need to know here." This immediately takes us out of the victim mentality and places us in the dominion God always intended.

The first Name that God revealed to me about himself was, "I am faithful. As long as you turn to me I will always be faithful to you."

When I found myself utterly alone in this huge world with a two year old and a seriously ill newborn...a baby who was always on the verge of dying...no money, no family, no help, no way to work because of the babies...I was finally without any human resources to "do it myself." I had to know that he was faithful and would care for us. Our literal survival depended on it. And he was. For three years I never worked and yet he arranged food, housing and all the needed essentials for living.

Because of this time, the name "faithful" was indelibly written upon my forehead. In every situation I have faced, in forty-eight years since then, my life was healed, corrected or whatever was needed appeared...simply because I carried the consciousness of the sure faithfulness of my God.

One such situation many years ago was my own healing of cervical cancer. When I was told those words I walked away and said with utmost confidence, "Well my life belongs to you and I am sure that whatever I need to know or do you will tell me." I was able to do this because his name, Faithfulness, was written upon my heart and mind. Four months later he told me...in spades! (Read *When the Wolf is at the Door*) And I was instantly healed. "He is faithful that promised. He cannot deny himself."[8] Besides the healing, the most incredible aspect of the whole experience to me was that I never felt fear and rarely thought about it for the four months prior to the healing. A true testament to Faithfulness imbedded within my consciousness.

Some years ago a very profound healing happened with my then six year old granddaughter. I received a call late one night from her mother, my second daughter, telling me that my granddaughter was in the back of an ambulance with her daddy being transferred to a Children's Hospital. She had been complaining of pain in her leg and when they x-rayed it they alluded to bone cancer, which would have meant an immediate amputation the next day. My understanding was that she was scheduled for surgery at 2:00 the next afternoon. Everything in my body and mind froze. The fear was excruciating. But as has always been my way, I prayed..."What do I need to know here?" In a second I saw the face of Jesus telling me that he was her...that there was only ONE of her...not two. Every time I saw her in my mind, he jumped in and said the very same words, "There are not two of her, just ONE." His face would replace her face in my mind. If I tell you that this happened hundreds of times that whole night, I would still be selling it short. It was constant. By the time I arrived at her bedside the next morning she was healed. The repeat x-rays were very normal, the blood work had returned to normal and her fever was gone. We took her home the next day, which incidentally was Thanksgiving Day. The chief surgeon looked at her mother and then at me and said, "Somebody in here was certainly praying."

But I wasn't praying. I was listening. I was hearing. And that actually has become praying to me. His name, ONENESS, was written eternally upon my forehead. No one could ever tell me that we were not one...that we aren't all the only begotten Son. The fullness of the revelation of the one, true God. This then is etched permanently within my eternal consciousness.

So then rather than weeping and wailing and asking God to heal...because healing to God is not fixing the visible problem but correction of the consciousness...we know he is faithful, so we just let him speak...let him teach...let him reveal. Every experience of an adversarial nature is to correct consciousness...because all the issues of life proceed from that unseen realm of knowing.

Recently I found myself in a heated conflict with someone. I was disturbed by the sudden and insidiousness of the attack. So I retreated to a quiet place and closed my eyes. "What do I need to know here?" The answer again was immediate. "I am Jehovah. That is my name." Jehovah speaks of God who always reigns supreme in wars or conflicts of any kind. Not choosing sides of right or wrong, but subduing and healing.

In minutes the winds began to change and the healing began. This was one of those conflicts that oftentimes never do get healed. And yet in minutes the change began. It was so impressive to me that forever I knew I now possessed that name. It would remain forever awakened in my soul.

So what I have learned through all these years is that instead of the focus being to wiggle and squirm trying to be extricated from a problem, situation, disease or whatever...instead of crying and wailing and wringing my hands...pacing and praying, my attention now is to turn away from the threat and go to that secret place within where my faithful God is present to write upon my forehead, etch within my heart, yet another faucet of his holy name. Building his house, by his Spirit, brick by brick, timber by timber, closer and closer to the eternal experience of being ONE with him.

CHAPTER SIX

KNOWING GOD BY NAME

God becomes much more intimate to us and far more accessible when we refer to him by a specific name. We know then exactly what we are needing and expecting to receive. The word God often brings up untrue images of anger, exacting, judging, distant and impossible to fully please, not to mention the progenitor of all human sufferings! But when we begin to know him by the specific attributes and true characteristics of his nature, we feel much closer and certainly more confident. Long ago I forsook calling him by the name God. It was just too distant and too cold for me. People who clearly have no clue as to his true nature blame the worst kind of horror on him, calling them "acts of God." Try as I might to dismiss all that, it yet would creep into my consciousness and undermine my trust and certainty.

At some point I was introduced to a specific religion that actually "broke down" some of the names of God. For instance it opened my heart to realize God as the Spirit of

Life. My study of God as Life was profound for me. It led me to learn to see beyond the visible appearances deep into the Life of every living thing. Persons, animals, creatures, plants, trees, birds, fish...good or bad, healthy or sick, angry or peaceful, criminal or saint...all came from the same "Source" (another name) and all possessed the Life we call God. Oneness. I found that if I chose to see that instead of what was appearing, if I took the moment to recognize it, bless it, exalt it...immediate changes, sometimes astonishing changes appeared. It was the first time I actually realized how and where this illusive Oneness would appear.

From there I went to the name Eternal Life. I found that eternity goes both ways. That I actually have always been in existence long before I arrived here and that I would remain alive within this experience called eternal Life forever. Death and the fear of it began to lose its grip and finally fade out of the picture altogether.

The name Immutable began to present itself. The unchangeable One. Nothing we think, believe, do or don't do will ever change the fact that I am his Life and his Life is what animates me. It sent me here. One day it will carry me home. I can't disengage myself from this if I wanted to...and who would?

Putting the name Eternal Life and Immutability together introduced me to a startling revelation. I didn't leave this Life behind when I arrived. I couldn't have. It has always been who I am, always led and guided me, never to be separated from it. Once again driving home for me the correction of what I grew up hearing...religion again telling us we "fell from it" and needed to gain it back through suffering, through a series of religious exercises, and then maybe if we are the lucky ones we might gain what we lost. Newsflash! We never lost it! All the power, authority, knowledge, wisdom, understanding...all that God is we have and do eternally possess. Immutable!

These names of God now are forever "written upon my forehead." My conscious awareness.

Then came the Spirit of Mercy. For two or three years I thought of little else. Any remnants of a god of wrath, judgment, anger, disappointment...exacting endless rules of behavior, was washed away. I began to study the Tabernacle that Moses erected in the wilderness journey. I found the Mercy Seat deep within the inner recesses of that structure. This taught me that the heart of our God is Mercy! Mercy is the Spirit given ability to, again, see beyond what is visible, deep into the soul of ourselves or another, and there find the immutable Goodness (another name) that is God. Within that name is the power to utterly wipe away all offenses causing us to shine forth in his nature. I learned what Jesus meant when he spoke to the very self-righteous religious leaders, "I will have Mercy and not endless religious sacrifices. Go and learn what that means!"[1] Well spoke James when he said, "Mercy rejoiceth against judgment!"[2]

Going back to the Mercy seat, I found that the Shekinah Glory that bursts forth from that Presence is actually a feminine name, speaking of God as both male and female. ("Let us make man in our image and after our likeness. Male and female made he them.")[3] The idea of a feminine Nature of God spoke to me of a heart so sensitive to our needs, so patient with our failures, compassionate, tenderhearted, easy to be entreated. Mercy lifts us to the Christ consciousness, our true identity...while judgment enshrouds us with more of a sense of condemnation and failure. This, my friends, is not our God. If there is any "wrath of God" at all, it would be against anything that appeared to "steal, kill or destroy us."[4] Never, never against us.

All this came from the study of just a few of the names of God. Revelation upon revelation. Closer and closer to that state of Oneness. But hearing and believing are one thing. Coming face to face with any of the Names of God is entirely another. Experiencing the immediate changes in situations and conditions because of "feeling" the Presence of a Name will forever write that nature upon your heart and cause you to become that name. John tells us that the Spirit and the Truth (the Word) "must agree." To only hear the truth, even over and over, without the experience of actually entering into it, will not be able to cause you to enter into that state of Oneness with it. Study it. Meditate upon it. Ask for greater understanding of it. Press in.

In the early years I grabbed hold of the name, Wisdom. In my youth I was always quick to react, leaving me defeated and always in some conflict or another. I reached out to the Spirit of Wisdom for correction. I read and re-read the book of Proverbs over and over until I nearly memorized it. It wasn't too long until I could feel myself being able to pause and wait a second before reacting... sometimes it required much more time than a second. I learned not to be impulsive with decisions and to patiently wait for Wisdom to speak. I felt so much more in control once I learned that. My confidence grew. I knew Wisdom would always lead me to do the right thing, to speak the right words, to enjoy the best results. Soon I was so confident that Wisdom and Sound Judgment (another name) was forever written upon my soul. I would always find the Guidance and Counsel (more names) that I would ever need. I listened and I learned from the Spirit of Understanding, the Spirit of Revelation, of the wonders of the person of God...my Father, my Source, and the Lover of my soul. While I am grateful for the many enlightened souls that have crossed my path and imparted the understanding they have accrued, the Holy Spirit is my one true teacher and guide.

The Islam religion has isolated over eighty "names" of God, realizing the importance of "knowing" God in an intimate way, (*Islam*, by Karen Armstrong) knowing the deepest aspects of his being, his purposes and intentions. Incidentally the word Islam means "to surrender." In its pure form it embraces Jesus as the sum total of all the names of God, the fullness of God. As do I.

When we realize that all the names of God collectively is actually the Holy Spirit, we begin to understand the imperative significance of the Holy Spirit towards us and its activity within us. We begin to understand the absolute dependence we must have upon its Presence and workings in order for the revelations that are needed and the bringing forth within us of the "one true man."

Jesus' words in the book of John first began to drive home to me the real function of the Holy Spirit and the individual "Spirits" contained within it. He realized that without the Presence of the Spirit "doing the works" they just wouldn't get done. He was aware enough of this and humble enough to surrender to the "impulse" of Spirit throughout his ministry here. He spoke only as he felt directed. He healed only when the Spirit was present to actually move across the "waters" of the consciousness of the individual needing healing, thereby correcting perception and understanding. He retreated often after a day of being thronged by folks in need so that he could replenish the Presence of the Spirit.

King David did the same thing. He would never move without "contacting the Spirit of Wisdom and Understanding" to go before him showing him the way. Even when to you and me the answer seemed obvious, yet he humbled himself before the purposes of God by asking and always obeying. The one or two times he didn't, the consequences were grave and his repentance was deeply felt. (Bringing home the Arc of the Covenant and the situation with Bathsheba.) Contrast this with Saul (symbolic of man under the mortal covering) who became impatient waiting for the revelation of God and "ran ahead of the Spirit" several times. He listened to the voices of others and the pressure they placed upon him. He failed to prove his obedience to God alone (humble heart before God) and he "lost" the kingdom. The story of Saul and David is a perfect contrast between living out from the mortal identity (mass consciousness) and living out from the immortal, Christ identity (Christ consciousness).

It is the Holy Spirit who causes us to desire to know the will of God, and hear the direction, and remain humble and trusting enough to wait and obey. This is the greatest lesson we can learn. This time here is not about us! It's not about the houses, the lands, the success, the perfect marriage, the talented kids, the money, power and prestige we accrue. We attempt to "use" God to secure these things...and he freely gives us what we desire...yet at the end of the day we find "leanness unto our souls."[5] To seek first the kingdom of God and the will and way of the Lord for each situation is to find all of the above and spiritual fulfillment and indescribable peace and joy as well...the kingdom within.

The certainty of the promise that God, whose name is Faithful, will send the Spirit before us and make the crooked ways straight, bring down the lofty mountains that stand before us boasting of their power to destroy, make a straight path to follow and cause the desert to blossom as the rose garden...is absolute. Call upon this for any and every situation you face and take a step back for a minute until you feel it happening. Then follow. "You shall hear a word behind you saying, 'This is the way, walk ye in it when you turn to the right hand or the left.'"[6] The meek and humble of heart will hear. Because they asked! There is no other qualification.

CHAPTER SEVEN

REMOVING THE SEALS
THE REVEALING OF JESUS CHRIST

About three years ago I felt compelled to read the Book of Revelation. I was cautioned not to try to understand it, just read it through every day that I could. Many folks have tried to explain it and the truth is it cannot be understood by the mind. It was written by the Spirit and can only be understood by the Spirit. If you still hold an ounce of belief that God is the progenitor of human suffering, and that we are either being punished or need it for our own good...then don't even attempt to read it until you know Him as pure Mercy..."never dealing with us after our iniquity." "Not imputing iniquity unto us."[1] Until you have left behind the "foundation of dead works" (Hebrews 6:1) and moved on up Jacob's Ladder to view the glory of being clean, pure and perfect in His sight, by the understanding of the New Covenant, (Hebrews, chapters 8,9,10)...then wait and read and understand that first. Until you have stood before the Great Throne of Mercy and realized that Mercy is the covering that removes all other defiling coverings, "for His Name sake," then you would be ready to read this work. The temptation is great to try to understand it, but wait for the Spirit of Revelation to pierce the veil and awaken your heart. It is worth the wait. The book of Revelation, as it states in Chapter 1, deals with the systematic revealing of Jesus Christ, through each one of us. For since the beginning he, the invisible expression of the fullness of God, has been within us...concealed under the debris of layers of mortal teachings and beliefs and errors of understandings "for of his fullness have we all received."[2]

Once more, the most important thing to understand is that this entire book, as well as the entire Bible, is about you, about me. It is the progressive awakening to who we really are, why we have come and what needs to be done. Each individual soul as it emerges from chaos and confusion into the Light of Eternal Life. The book of Revelation is no different. It speaks of Jesus, the Lamb, removing the seven seals that hide the Glory of God. Again seven being a symbolic number. The Lamb is Jesus, of course, but it is also you and I, as we willingly take on the nature of a lamb, becoming meek, submissive, yielding, following, trusting and obeying the Shepherd of our souls. That is why it can only be the lamb who can remove the seals. The lamb nature emerging from the recesses of the soul. The lamb, who never runs ahead of the Shepherd, but always trusts enough to follow.

The second thing that must be understood is that the "wrath" you will read about is never against you, but always against the evil influences, the layers of coverings that have held the souls in the bondage of misery and suffering for so long. You are now and have always been held safe in the heart of Love...and as soon as the heart turns towards eternal Love, it realizes this and is quiet and at rest.

The seals are like the layers of an onion, with each layer removed, the darkness, the lies and distortions of truth, etc. are released...but remember we are not hurt! The only thing destroyed is the destroyer...the chaotic mortal way of reasoning and thinking. We are "sealed" with the protection of the Holy Spirit until we are finally free to be released as the Glory of God revealed.

So the true "second coming" is when the Only Begotten, many membered Son is revealed through us and "God is seen to be all in all!"[3] From the revealing of the great Throne Room (chapter 4) deep within your soul ("The kingdom of God is within you,")[4] till the emerging of the new heaven and the new earth (chapter 20-22). It is all about each one of us, as though there were only one of us. The new heaven is when his name, (our new name) is fully impressed upon our consciousness, written on our forehead, and the new earth is the visible manifestation of it all.

Chapter after chapter we read about the removal of the "seals or coverings," until the garment worn is as white as new fallen snow. The issue is with those seals or coverings...there is no issue with you. Until at the end of the removals, when Babylon is fallen...(the word Babel means the confusion of many voices or influences)...and all human insanity and hysteria has been swallowed up.

Remember it is speaking of the individual consciousness of man as well as the collective consciousness of man. This is the appearing of the new heaven (consciousness) and the new earth (visible appearances). This is the awakening to the One New Man, and just as the first chapter declares, this is the revelation of Jesus Christ...through you. Through me.

It was during this time and through this reading that heaven, (God, Jesus, eternity) shifted from "out there" to deep within my own being. This shift must take place at some point for each one. "He broke down the middle wall of partition making of the two one new man."[5] Forever gone now is the sense of separation between myself and God, the sense of duality. Now there is one, no longer two.

No matter how it happens for each one, we must know this...it can only happen through the workings of the Holy Spirit. The mind cannot begin to grasp this. It can know about it. It can read about it. It can talk about it, sing about it and repeat it until the world becomes flat. But it can only happen by the Spirit of God...grace (the activity of the Spirit in the heart of men).

This is the beginning of the experience of Oneness. This is the beginning of the re-appearance of Jesus Christ. This is him coming in the clouds and we, in our mortality, are the clouds, blocking the fullness of the Glory of God.

Jesus prayed that we would come into the experience of Oneness, even as he did, knowing that without the sense of eternity within us, we could not "work the works of him that sent us."[6] We would never realize the earth being "filled with his Glory as the waters cover the sea!"[7]

Gaining this overpowering sense of everything we read about actually taking place deep in our own souls, ultimately gives us that sense of authority over all the works of darkness for ourselves and others.

I think the beginning of knowing God as Eternal Life...a Life with no beginning and no ending... and me, as having been a part of that since before the beginning of the world and forever and ever...was the beginning of this extreme shift that has taken place over the past few years. I began to feel myself as an eternal being...more and more of the sense of mortality and subsequent victimhood dissolving before me.

Reading the 4th chapter of Revelation would send my soul soaring, my heart tripping along with the excited sense of wonderment.

Quoting some of the 4th chapter, we read in part, "and immediately I was in the spirit and behold a throne was set in heaven, and ONE sat on the throne." "And out of the throne proceeded lightening's and thundering's and voices. And there were seven lamps of fire burning before the throne, which are the seven spirits of God..." "And these spirits rest not day nor night crying, 'Holy, Holy, Holy Lord God almighty, heaven and earth are full of your Glory.'"

We are told that we are seated at the right hand of this throne. With all power and authority given to us in heaven and earth. All other so-called powers are now under our feet.[8] We are "in him who is the Lamb"[9] telling us that the Spirit of humility is highly exalted with God.

To begin to finally feel a part of this, NOW, on earth

when we really need it most, is an achievement and an honor to the Spirit of God who "makes all things new!"[10]

Now throughout the removal of these seals, these spirits of God are "sent out" to do various things to facilitate this removal and the subsequent revealing of the Glory which lies beneath. In the high and exalted state of humility which we are oftentimes lifted to, we may also release a specific spirit of God to do a specific work and since this is the place of absolute authority, they will respond to the will and purpose and intention of God for every interaction with creation. For in this place we are all one.

So the coverings must go and we must commit to the Spirit our ways, our days, our struggles and challenges. As we turn to him, we are covered by the Spirit and kept safe till the offending influences are removed.

With each challenge, with each trusting moment, more of his name is written on our hearts. We come to know him in ways we only heard of before. As this progresses in our lives we really do begin to enter a place of peace, because we know him, as he truly is, and not as man has babbled through the centuries.

Examining now the more specific names of God, or spirits of God, we will find all of this to be as near to us as our breath…bridging the gap that has caused God to feel so distant from man.

CHAPTER EIGHT

THE SEVEN SPIRITS OF GOD

The attributes, the many spirits of God, are probably as vast as the oceans and as many as the stars of heaven. I will break down a few to give the general idea of what is specifically being referred to here. Once you begin to identify some of these yourselves, and see them working in your lives, you will realize how much closer, how much more intimate is your understanding of God. You will find yourself more secure and confident in your lives...as trusting becomes easier.

The Spirit of God as the Creative Principle: We all know God is the Creator of the heavens and earth and all that is contained within. But knowing that information just doesn't bring him, in that capacity, closer to me. As time went by I began to see this creative energy (spirit) not as something that did its work and then drifted away from us, but rather as someone whose Presence actually maintains and sustains the perfection and immutability of it all. Very important.

I think of the Spirit mostly as a river. A river flowing to and through me with intention and purpose. As the divine intention to bring forth into visible expression is released, something is created. It is given form out from the imagination of intention. (Mind of God) It is always created out from the Being of God and therefore regardless of what it turns out to be, it will contain all that God is. That includes every aspect of creation. Everything formed in some way speaks of him whose intention formed it. From the infinitesimal to the infinite. It comes from perfection and holiness, and it remains so throughout eternity.

So if in our perception we look upon something imperfect, does God need to re-create it to make it right? No! Of course not. It is we who need our perception, our understanding, our vision corrected. People who speak of "being co-creators with God" think that God is running around re-creating something. Fixing something that is broken. And that he needs us to help in this frantic process. They need to refresh their memory of the chapters at the end of Job when God assures Job that he was well able to create without his help. That, in fact, he needed no help from anyone anywhere!

Everything is as it has been created, perfect, whole and complete. "For you are complete in him."[1]

The names of God here are several. One is the Spirit of Understanding. One is the Spirit of Truth. Another is the Spirit of Immutability. Immutability again is absolute unchangeableness. Looking again at Ecclesiastes 3:14, "everything God has made shall be forever; nothing can be added to it and nothing taken from it." So in fact nothing ever needs to be fixed! All that is needed is our unwavering acceptance of what is! Right in the face of a lying distortion of the truth.

If the truth were to be known, right here, right now the whole earth is filled with the Glory of God as the waters cover the sea.[2] Otherwise he would not be Omnipresent (another name). If something could distort what the Creative Principle has formed, then he would not be Omnipotent (another name).

Truth is not simply words of profound understandings. Although this is certainly the first needed stepping stone. Truth stored in the mind is needed but not able to change a hair on our head.[2] The truth must be felt in consciousness, in the feeling part of the soul. The Spirit of Truth (another name) takes the words of truth and penetrates the inner fabric of your being. Now they are real. Now you have seen the results of knowing instead of simply hearing. Now you carry this name throughout eternity.

When faced with any adversity, any appearance of destruction or the threat of destruction, the first thing to remember is that Life cannot be interrupted. It is the essence of the entire God-Being. So this picture before you is just this and nothing more...it is a projection of the beliefs of men, coming to you for recognition and validity. Do not give it!

Stand still. Stand firm. When alone ask God for direction in prayer, such as, "What must I see here? What is the immutable truth here?" When we begin to clearly feel what is true, we have just encountered the Spirit of Truth. It is now forever etched upon our consciousness. It is an aspect of the Name that is forever ours.

What made this happen? First, you realized that all the babbling and repeating and insisting on the words of truth will never bring the needed change. Because it is not in "man" to do these things. Never with the mind of man, never with the efforts of man will anything in consciousness be corrected. Only by the flow of the Spirit of Truth! So in recognition of this and with the deepest humility we ASK for the Spirit of Guidance, the Spirit of Revelation, the Spirit of Truth, itself, to teach us, show us, flow through us, writing upon our hearts the fullness of his name.

The story of the Prodigal Son[4] is a classic example of us, as the sons of God, thinking we can make it happen with our own efforts. Turning away from our father's house (Divine Mind, Consciousness) and figuring it all out by things we have only heard. But once humility covers our wandering hearts and we cry out for our father house, (the mind and heart of God) the feeling of the truth appears...and all things now appear new.

All through the Israelites' wanderings through the wilderness they met and battled one nation after another. Each one of these nations have a particular meaning. To name a few, the Canaanites and Perizzites mean strife and division: the Amorites mean self-love, self-exaltation. The Hittites mean hate, while the Hivites mean fear. You will notice that these, and many others besides, all refer to the many challenges we all face as we make our way through the maze of our wilderness experience, the human consciousness.

But the one nation that they continually ran up against were the Moabites. Around every corner, so to speak, were those persistent Moabites. Moab was one of the sons born to Lot and his daughters from an incestual relationship.[5] The meaning of the Moabites is doing exactly what Lot's daughters did...and that was trusting in their own efforts to bring forth a desired result. We have two choices here. We either remember what we know is true and think that by many insistencies and repeatings we can correct something. Or we can stop. Put on the brakes and ask for the Spirit of direction, the Spirit of guidance to fill our heart with the spirit of the truth. Then and only then is the problem corrected. But even more than this, it is forever a part of our new consciousness, the house that God is building.

Have you ever felt attacked in your life? Has anyone verbally attacked you? Have you felt judged, condemned, shut out? Have you ever been really unjustly accused? The important thing is not to attack back. Immature people think they won if they can attack back. They love to repeat what they said that "put the other guy in his place." First of all this is an opportunity for you to exercise restraint. It is an opportunity for you to see the Spirit of Advocacy rise up and stand before you in your defense. You won't see him. You just need to know he is there. Call upon him. Know that he is standing before you. Know that he is dealing with those who suddenly became your enemy. Let him do his work. Your job is to not rehearse the situation. Not hold onto it. Call upon Grace to calm your heart and enable you to hold the perfection of the person in consciousness. Insist upon it. You won't feel it, you may not see it yet...but it's there nevertheless. If you are faithful to do this, soon there will be peace (another name) restored. You will be elevated and set in honor by this Advocate you now know as being very real. Remember the goal of God is Oneness. He will not rest until this is realized by all parties. God fights our battles if we let him and are faithful to the truth as best as we know it.

It's impossible to get through this life without at some point suffering a loss so great that the grief seems to consume you. But the Spirit of the Comforter is standing before you waiting to carry that grief away. The Provider is there ready to fill in the space that was lost to you. There is no shame in tears. They are needed. But to continue carrying the pain is unnecessary and unproductive. I thought when my sister and brother-in-law died that I would never stop screaming inside. The pain was crushing to me. The loss was great. For a long time I held onto it. I forgot to allow the Comforter to carry away the pain. I forgot to allow the great Provider to fill in the space left by them. What I went through was of no value to me or anyone else. You probably think that nothing can ever take it away, but you think that because you have not asked and allowed it to happen. Like anything else, as soon as you ask with all your heart, Grace is there to deliver.

I knew a man who was in business with his best friend from school days. He was probably in his seventies when I met him, so they had been best friends and business partners almost as long. One day he realized his friend was embezzling the finances and stealing the business away from him. By the time he saw it, it was too late to recover. In the depths of his grief he became sick with cancer. I told him that God would heal him of this betrayal. But he couldn't believe that it was possible. He just never did ask. I told him God would fill the space that was lost, but he thought he was too old for anything else to come his way. So he died in his pain. This is why it is so very important for us to know him by name. It gives us the kind of confidence that says, "Of course God will do this. I know this is his nature."

Even though we cannot see a possible way out there is always one. Even though we cannot imagine anything better, there always is...just waiting for us to open our hearts and trust. Just ask. "Taste of me and see that I am good."[6] Give God the chance to prove his name, his faithfulness, his provisions, his comfort, his grace to you. This is the time to let it appear and know him as you never knew him before. He will forever write these names on your heart.

You can see that the trials and crises we face can be used to destroy us or to elevate us to another conscious realization of the person of God, an intimate knowing him, as well as a correction in the human appearance. We have a choice to turn to him, even in doubt, fear, cynicism, or whatever defense we throw up...the idea is to turn to him anyway. He will deliver. Even now as always, the Spirit of God in all its many properties is surrounding you, stirring within you, calling you to "learn of me."[7]

CHAPTER NINE

OUR HIGH CALLING, PT. 1

Revelation, chapter 5:10, says that we are called to be kings and priests unto our God. "He has made us unto our God, kings and priests...and we shall reign on the earth."

This is critical information and must be clearly understood and embraced.

People often ask me, when all this is finally realized what will we be doing? When Oneness is fully achieved and realized in the individual consciousness, kings and priests will be our role.

Oneness is clearly defined in Ephesians, chapter 2:14, and worthy of repeating, "he is our peace who has made of both one and has broken down the middle wall of partition making of the two, one new man." The veil between the mortal and the immortal, deep within each soul is removed by the death of one man, who stood as us all, burying the one that the other might be manifested. The one thing you want to notice is that it is done. It is now just a matter of it being clearly seen and felt in each heart. The mortal is now a manifestation of the immortal. Divinity has supplanted humanity and is manifested through humanity. Heaven on earth. "For this mortal must put on immorality, this corruptible must put on incorruption."[1] Although this is already achieved, each individual consciousness must experience it. And when it does the role of King and Priest will automatically be the nature realized.

In the meantime, the Bible says that God will bless our "goings in and comings out."[2] But later we read that the time will come when we will "go in and come out no longer."[3] Until that day comes we still can, and need, to perform the offices of King and Priest whenever we find ourselves in that exalted state.

I have heard people say that when there is Oneness we will all love each other. This is not a "Kumbaya" doctrine. This is not the reason for Oneness being achieved. We are called to be elevated in consciousness unto the eternal fulfillment of God's purpose and intention for sending us here. It will be as Jesus spoke, "On earth as it is in heaven."[4] "God will be seen to be all in all."[5] This experience needs to be kept on a level between all that God is and us. It is not to be "used" for any specific human goal. No matter how noble that goal is. My human goal would be to see the day that the imagination of mass hysteria over our bodies, disease, aging and the like is completely annihilated. But I can't look at that. Why? Because if that was my goal and vision, that would still be the level of my consciousness. Nothing of the human consciousness can enter into the Paradise of God. It is impossible to take any human thought or problem "into the gates of Jerusalem on the Sabbath day."[6] And that alone would keep me from entering in. Thus the angel with the flaming sword[7] is faithful to burn away, cut away, any motive or thought contrary to the purity of this most holy place deep within us. The vision, the heart must be toward the fullness of God alone. All the rest will certainly follow.

Let's look at the function of a king.

Obviously it is one who rules over a kingdom. It is one who reigns supreme. His word is the law. It is not up for argument or for dispute. The king doesn't wring his hands wondering if what he says will be done. He knows it will. So there is a confidence, a certainty about him. He knows that "none of his words will fall to the ground, but will accomplish that for which they have been sent out. They will never return to him void."[8]

The very first commandment given to us is to "take dominion and subdue the earth."[9] This refers to the whole of the "earth consciousness" or what we call mass consciousness. It is a consciousness which "reacts" to whatever imagination of man that is prevalent at the moment. It is governed by fear. It sees only through the eyes of darkness and it is constantly jumping through the hoop of "but what if..." God's answer to that is, "Why do you cry aloud, is there no king in you?"[10] Never let a thought of disbelief enter your mind. It will happen. You will reign as king. "Say not in thine heart, 'Who will reach up to heaven and bring this down for me?' For the word of faith is nigh thee in thine heart and in thine mouth."[11]

Contrast that with the response (not reaction) to one

who is under the covering of the Holy Spirit. When under the covering of the human consciousness, the mortal identity, we are always reacting to whatever is appearing. This is the victim mentality. But when under the covering of the Holy Spirit, we respond, because we know we are safe and only need to hear and obey in every situation. Living out from the "house that God has built." Following only the directions and impulses of Spirit. One who has learned not to "jump" because the world says, "Jump!" But is solid, steadfast and has "learned obedience by the many challenges faced in their lifetime."[12] One who knows that "humility breeds Divinity." One who has become comfortable with the sound of the Voice and has experienced the healings, and corrections and blessings of following that voice...as well as the disasters of failing to heed. One who has been taught of the Spirit how to be a faithful ruler over the kingdom, one that can be trusted. Oneness is proven when we take on the role of one who is superior to all human conditions and therefore able to subdue them. This must be a house built by God alone. We certainly wouldn't know where to start, otherwise.

Now Proverbs says that the king is to rule over his own city. "He that has no rule over his own spirit is like a city that is broken down and without walls."[13] That city is our soul, the innermost consciousness of each person. We also read that "when the righteous are in authority the people rejoice. But when the wicked beareth rule, the people mourn."[14] The only place we need to concern ourselves with is what we are holding in our own consciousness. We perceive life from that alone.

When we run into a problem, any major or minor threat, we try to fix it where it has appeared. But it actually comes from what we hold in consciousness. If you're at a movie theater and something goes wrong with the picture, no one runs up and tries to fix the screen. The problem is within the projector behind the scenes. When that is corrected, the picture "out there" will have an entirely different appearance.

There is a familiar Hawaiian healing prayer we talk about here. It is called Ho'oponopono. It is very effectual. There are four steps to this healing treatment.

1. "I'm sorry."
2. "Please forgive me."
3. "Thank you."
4. "I love you."

What exactly are we saying we're sorry about? For seeing something that God never ordained. For being an unfaithful projector.

We begin to heal it by first becoming aware of it and then repenting for it. When we hold something in consciousness that is of a destructive nature we are denying the all-ness of God. We are also blocking the flow of the Spirit of God from within. Like a muddy screen keeping the sunlight from getting through.

Several years ago I received a phone call from a very distraught grandmother. Her four year old grandson was going back to surgery for the second time for a removal of a malignant brain tumor. "Would you please pray that it's not there?" Well I knew I couldn't pray that way but I assured her that I would pray. For forty-five minutes I stayed with the "I'm sorry" phase of the treatment. I said I was sorry to this little boy forever acknowledging such a monstrous thing could exist. I was sorry for every doctor and nurse who also acknowledged this. For every person who ever spoke it. Believed it. Taught it. Wrote about it. Or ever thought they or someone else had it. Mostly for his family who clung to the very image they prayed would "go away." By holding these "in"-graven images in thought we all allowed a very destructive covering over him. Thus the depth of the "I'm sorry" phase.

I chose to "rule over my city." I chose to be the king. Since we are all one being, I knew deep in his consciousness he received my words. Thus the "please forgive me" and the thank you" phase of the treatment. The next call I received several days later told me that when they got to the operating room and took pictures before the surgery started, the tumor was not there. It never appeared again.

The king is instructed to have "no false gods before him."[15] Nothing that he gives power to other than the One God, Supreme. He is to have "no graven image" before him. Nothing "in"-graven, interwoven within the fabric of his soul introduced by the mass consciousness of mortality. He was sent here to "subdue and take dominion over all the works of darkness."[16] Surprisingly enough once it's cleared from within, it is cleared period. This causes us to lose the false concept of "chance."

Years ago I came upon a problem within my own family. One member of my family would be classified as an alcoholic. After wasting a few years fretting, I decided to "see" this person only as the Only Begotten Son, Jesus. I held to it no matter what I saw, no matter what I heard. And very soon there was an overwhelming, significant improvement. But a few short years later it was back again. I asked God what I was missing and the answer was quick to appear. The belief that a man made in the image of God could be overwhelmingly addicted to something was strong in my own consciousness, as I had been raised by alcoholic parents. Now it was time to finally deal with that issue. I knew it was no match for me, but was entirely within the scope of the office of the Holy Spirit to dig it out and wash away any remaining image of such. Once the "void" was established in consciousness, I knew he would fill the space with the true image of man in the image of God, manifesting the only begotten son. I was certain of it. And that is exactly what happened. No human effort. Just laying the whole thing at the feet of the Spirit of God. The worst of all human conditions respond to this every time. "Judgment begins at the house of the Lord."[17]

False ideas of the nature of God are also graven images. If we hold in consciousness that God is the progenitor of evil, of suffering or the like, we will never be able to live a life devoid of suffering. But if we would spend less time trying to fix the suffering that has appeared and more time learning the nature of the Most Holy One, getting at the root of the issue, we would be delivered from what we are presently experiencing and begin to live a life of pure goodness, free of fear of what may happen.

In the mortal identity we live as victims, coming under the law of chance. We never know what might appear to hurt from one day to the next. So unknowingly we stay in a state of being guarded and tense. The most exalted state of consciousness of the king is to do what I call, "turn it around." When faced with any adversarial condition or situation, if I just stop in my tracks and remember that I am the king of the kingdom of God and I have been "sent" to this image of disaster, or whatever, to subdue it and be in a state of dominion over it. Therefore I am superior to this picture and if I know it...it knows it also!

I have an immediate choice to make: Either I am a victim of this and now I need to find a way out, or I remember that it did not come to me to hurt or destroy because it can't. No! I was sent to it. Deliberately and for the purpose of subduing it and removing it. Did it come to me or am I sent to it? Nothing immediately lifts me out of being a victim and places me in a state of superiority than the correct answer to this.

Remember that the whole cleansing of the "city," as well as the maintenance of the newly established divine order, is a work of the Spirit. The minute we think there is something we need to do, we have removed it from his capable hands and wasted a lot of time. Let us choose to come under the covering of the Spirit of God "that it might go well with us" all the days of our lives...as a king unto God.

CHAPTER TEN

OUR HIGH CALLING, PT. 2

There are two entire books in the Old Testament (Exodus and Leviticus) which speak of the priesthood. This is the significance that God places upon this divine intention. As is the case throughout the Old Testament, the role of the priest can only be understood by the revelation of the Holy Spirit. Every garment, every sacrifice, every oblation, every holy day, every animal used for the sacrifices, all carry a deeply significant spiritual meaning for us today. The New Testament book of Hebrews declares that all things written in the Old Testament are types and shadows of heavenly things to come...not able to be understood until the coming of the Holy Spirit, who alone is able to reveal these things unto us.

And we have this calling and honor...that we are formed and sent here to be such a priest unto God. The fulfillment of this is altogether a work of the Spirit within us, as we yield ourselves to it.

Ezekiel, chapter 44, speaks of two kinds of priesthood.

The one most common to us "stands before the people to minister to them," the focus being the churches, the congregants and all the issues surrounding them. While they may be devoted to their work and to God, they fail to enter into the office of the Most Holy Priesthood. This often produces an emptiness within that cannot be explained.

But the true priest "stands before the Lord to minister to him alone." Thus he is able to fulfill the reason for the priesthood in the first place. This service is done alone and in quietness, for it is solely between the one acting now as priest and the God of Mercy. When this is followed as outlined by the Spirit, we will find we have the privilege of being able to reconcile any person, or nation of peoples "back to the Lord." This means back to their original state of perfection and divinity.

And the fulfillment of this purpose is accomplished by forgiveness. But not the forgiveness we are accustomed to. This is not, "say your penance and your sins are forgiven. This is not, "I forgive you of this offense you have committed." This does not deal on the horizontal plane from person to person at all.

But first let me go back to what is required of this priest. When approaching the Presence of God, he is not to "wear anything that causes sweat."[1] He can take no concern for the person he is representing with him. This, I know, is difficult. It's hard to let go of the emotions that often accompany the person in trouble or the situation. But we must. The consciousness of the priest must be about honoring the truth of God, not giving power to anything that is exalting itself before the majesty of his holy Being. He must be free to be exalted into that Holy state of one who is once again about to perform a miracle. He is about to remove every sin (covering) that has attached itself to the Holy Son of God that is concealing his true identity. This is true forgiveness. The word forgiveness actually means to "send away," to remove. By doing so he is allowing that person to enter into that sacred place of the experience of "oneness" where they and their God become one and the same being...the greater swallowing up the lesser.

It was from this place that Jesus lived his life. It was from this place that he spoke such words of eternal wisdom. And it was from this place he healed and worked his miracles. This is the place that we must enter where "greater things than these shall you do also."[2] This is where we become one with, and as, the Only Begotten Son.

But here we must be cautioned...we can never accomplish this until our own consciousness is free of any judgment of the offense or fear of the disease...we cannot carry anything of a mortal nature with us into that place. If we find a "block" within as we approach this, we must pause and ask and realize what thoughts we, ourselves, are holding here. We must repent if we are giving power to the problem by acknowledging it a power. We must allow the Spirit to move across our souls and sweep away whatever we are holding onto. We may not know what it is but the Spirit does, and it must go. This Spirit is "quick and powerful and sharper than any two edged sword, piercing even to the dividing of soul and spirit...and the joints and marrow, and is a discerner of the thoughts and intents (motives) of the heart."[3] I often say that the far majority of the work is this phase within my own soul...once this is done, the remaining treatment is simple.

Another requirement is that the priest carry with him the "fat and the blood"[4] into the Presence of God. The fat is the oil and the oil is always the Holy Spirit. He is declaring by doing so that this is totally a work of Spirit and not a work of man. He is waiting on the Spirit to move across the waters of his soul and lead the way. The blood is the Life. "The Life is in the blood."[5] This declares that there is but One Life and he knows that underneath all the coverings that, and that only, remains untouched, uninterrupted and immutable. This must be foremost in the consciousness of the priest. It is the lifting of this awareness in the consciousness of the one being prayed for that actually does the healing.

Another necessary requirement of the priest in order to fulfill his office, is that he has a deep understanding and revelation of the nature of God as Mercy. So what is mercy exactly? Let me tell you first what mercy is not. It is not compassion. It is not empathy. It is not comfort. It is not a free pass or a license to transgress. As a matter of fact, "by mercy and truth iniquity is purged."[6]

Mercy is the divine ability to see beyond the mortal to the true man that never changes. When that takes place...the true man emerges. All false coverings disappear. This is Divine Love's way of freeing man from the enslavement of sin and disease. Not suffering. Not punishment. This is contrary to the ignorant ranting of the ugly voice of religions throughout the world and throughout generations. Punishment might make the transgressor stop what they are doing, but it leaves them in condemnation, unable to heal them at the level of consciousness. "The strength of sin is condemnation." Without Mercy cleansing the consciousness, they may "get over" the situation, but the same consciousness remains present to allow another situation to appear.

This was the very reason the New Covenant was brought forth. Man could never correct himself or others by human ways and means. But the appearing of the Holy Spirit, moving in the hearts of mankind could. And that is grace.

Again, we cannot become a true priest unto God without an understanding and revelation of mercy. Because mercy is the aspect of the nature of God that actually does it.

And how is this done? By forgiveness. And again, it is not the same forgiveness we have heard about forever. One person forgiving another for an offense. This is way beyond that because that can never make the consciousness of the individual enter into that very necessary state of wholeness..."having a consciousness void of offense both toward God and man."[7] This is healing the hearts and consciousness of the people through mercy. This is standing in the Presence of Mercy itself in behalf of another until we are able to actually "feel" the person as the Holy Son of God. Only the spirit can enable us to see beyond the oftentimes hideous images of sin and disease. (In ourselves as well.) Only the spirit can enable us to feel the presence of the Holy Son of God within them. This is true forgiveness. This is what Jesus was referring to when he breathed on them and said, "Receive the Holy Spirit. Whosoever sins you remit they are forgiven."[8]

As the children of Israel wandered through their wilderness experience they were spiritually sustained by many rituals, offerings, holy days and of course, by the presence of their place of worship, the Tabernacle that Moses erected. Once a year the High Priest took the blood of a lamb and entered "through the veil into the Most Holy Place."[9] There was the Presence of God. There was the Glory of God. There was the fullness of God in his Spirit and Life. This was called the Day of Atonement. This was the day when all debts were cancelled. When all sins were removed. When all prisoners were set free. This was a day of rejoicing, shouting and gladness never heard of in the earth before. They were free, free, free. It is said that their enemies heard the shouting from far away and knew better than to attempt to approach them.

What did the High Priest encounter there? Seated above the Ark of the Covenant and covered by two huge Cherubims was the Mercy Seat, the heart of God. He approached the eternal Mercy that wipes away all offense and reveals the one man made in the image of beauty and perfection and wholeness.

Instead of punishment man finds himself cleared of offenses, but also in a highly exalted state of being One with the fullness of God. Any tendency to re-cover one's self with the same offense would almost be preposterous. The eternal, divine intention is to reveal the fullness of God, through and as, his beloved Son. Not by whipping him into obedience, not by eternal suffering... all these doctrines only prove the blindness of the hearts of men as to the true nature and purpose of God. To repeat the words of Jesus, "I will have mercy and not sacrifice. Go and learn what that means!"[10] Mercy truly "rejoices against judgment."[11]

When we feel the impulse of Spirit to perform the office of the priest, we enter with confidence, being fully persuaded "that it is for this reason we have come."[12] It is for this reason we have been called and chosen and sent here at this very moment. This is always the will of God. "To set the captives free and that you break every yoke."[13] We remember that beyond the veil, the mortal coverings, we are all ONE as the only begotten son of God. This person, or persons, are his "masterpiece, created in perfection,"[14] and they carry the fullness of him that formed them and sent them.

We do this without words or cumbersome human thoughts. Of these things we are certain. And so we approach with confidence, with humility, with gratitude and with a certainty as to the outcome. Because this is our purpose, and the whole intention of God. We remain in silence until we feel the work is completed, remembering that "he performs that thing which is appointed for you to do."[15]

Because this is such a sacred space we visit, we do as Moses and change our garments and cover this moment so as not to expose the holy things of God to mortal thought. This means we don't talk about this experience to anyone along our way...until, and unless, we are so directed by the Spirit to do so.

Healing after healing will appear before you. Your "joy will be great."[16] And no man or situation will be able to take this from you.

CHAPTER ELEVEN

ONENESS REVEALED

The ultimate Divine intention is that darkness, ignorance, be swallowed up by understanding and the radiant light of Spirit. This is preordained and therefore will manifest on the earth. (As in heaven, so on earth.) Of this there is no doubt. This will be the "new heaven and the new earth" we read of in Revelation. Although this is a work of Spirit, there are attitudes of the heart and understandings of the mind that must cooperate with the workings of Spirit.

There are fundamental Christian doctrines upon which this is built. However, it is imperative that we ascend into a much greater understanding of these if we are to enjoy the state of Oneness we desire. As Oneness is realized within each individual we find ourselves, with no thought or effort, living superior to all human conditions...and easily enabling others to do the same. This is a progressive revealing and we can begin today.

ONE LIFE

Acts 17:26 "...and hath made of One Blood ("The life is in the blood") all nations of men to dwell on the face of the earth."

Life is not what we are doing. Life is not for personal possession. There is not "my life," "your life" or "their life." There are not multitudes of lives, even though that is what you see. There is only One Life. Just as there are multitudes of branches, twigs, leaves, nuts, fruit...yet one tree. One tap root. One Source.

There is one, eternal, perfect, intact Life. It has always been. It will always be. It flows as the Spirit of Life.

As it is the Creative Principle, it enjoys multitudes of formations, each with a unique manifestation of the One Life. Yet still only one life. "For the invisible things of him from the creation of the world are clearly seen, being understood by the things that are made, even his eternal power and Godhead."[1]

It is the substance that holds all things in their orbital order, from the infinitesimal to the infinite.

It is God. God being the life of all that is.

If this Spirit of Life were to be removed, the formations would cease to exist. But the Life would continue to flow...uninterrupted. It is eternal. It is incorruptible. It is undisturbed.

It is. And there is nothing except it that exists.

This will be the ultimate understanding...when we know that God is all there is. "...that God will be seen to be all and all."[2] "For of him and to him and through him are all things."[3] "That he will gather all things unto himself, things in earth, in heaven and under the earth."[4]

This is the "mystery of God, hid for all ages, but now ready to be revealed,"[5] spoken of by Paul. While we cannot make this appear, for this is the function of the Holy Spirit from beginning to end, we can come to understand and cooperate with our role. This will place us in a complete receptive mode, which is necessary for the fulfillment.

We must lose the sense of individual "me." We must learn to identify with that Life. The more we do, the less adversarial situations can appear. This will prove that "greater is that Life within you than anything else that boasts itself a power to interrupt it."[6]

Jesus was the complete expression of that life. He knew that "to lose his life"[7] (his sense of an independent life) was the answer to this Life freely appearing.

In John, chapter 12, when two Greeks came to meet him, they asked to "see" him. He knew that to see him within, and as, themselves was the true request, even though they couldn't have known that at the time. The only way to "see" him within is to connect with this eternal life that he manifested. Therefore his response was this…"Except a corn of wheat fall to the ground and die, it will abide alone. But if it dies it will bring forth much fruit. He that loves his life (individual and separate existence) will lose it, but he that does not cling to his life (but is willing to lose that sense of individual possession) will keep it throughout eternity."

To worship Jesus will never be enough. To lose our sense of individual life in order for him to appear (the fullness of God) is the only answer. This is the veil or covering "cast over all nations"[8] that we experience at our arrival. This is called the human consciousness or mortal identity. This is governed by the law of chance and manifests as total self-orientation. When this veil is transcended we will appear as the Glory of this Life...as we have always been. "He will destroy in this mountain (mortality) the face of the covering cast over all people. And death will be swallowed up in victory and he will wipe away tears from off of all faces."[9] "...neither sorrow nor crying, neither shall there be any more pain. For behold, I make all things new."[10]

We must know at some point that the veil no longer exists over us. It has already been swallowed up by Life. Any mortal response now is a reaction to a false idea, an idea that declares itself a power besides God and greater than God...as opposed to seeing through the eyes and heart of immutable God.

Now we react to projected imaginations only. "God has caused man to walk upright before him, but he has sought out many evil imaginations."[11]

At Jesus' death the blinding veil was "rent from top to bottom."[12] It was removed for all men for all time. How did this happen? Jesus represented the Only Begotten Son, of which we all are. When he prayed, "Father forgive them,"[13] he was acting as the High Priest for all mankind and at that point the veil, the coverings were forgiven..."sent away."

When he chose to let the covering of humanity, mortality, be once and forever removed and buried, we (all as one) experienced that. When he arose into immortality, we arose also as the only son.

Oneness, contrary to popular understanding, is not that we all will be of one mind, one heart, one spirit...although that will certainly appear. No. Oneness is all about each one of us individually and God. The entire sense of individuality, a separate existence from God...even God in us and we in him... will be replaced with the "experience" of God being all that is. Meaning all the names, attributes and characteristics...the complete Being as One. No more "he and me." Not two, but one. When this happens in the consciousness of the individual, the whole of creation will respond in the same knowing. For we are the covering of creation. As it goes with man so goes it for every animal, plant, bird and fish...all of creation.

And this will happen. For "he performs that thing which is appointed for me."[14]

One way Oneness is realized will be when we make a firm intention and agreement with "seeing" the Life within the form. If I can realize it as you, I can realize it as me. If I can accept it as me than it certainly is you as well. If I don't see it in another, the problem is that I am "judging after the seeing of my eyes and the hearing of my ears."[15] I am the one needing to have that area of the mortal consciousness replaced with truth. Then "out there" will take on another appearance.

Once again, if I am at a movie theater and something becomes blurry and distorted with the picture, I don't run up to the screen to straighten it out. I go back to the projector and fix the problem there.

Remember when Jacob went out to meet his brother Esau after years of separation and bitter hatred?[16] Jacob feared for his life. He prayed all night till the dawn broke (the light in his soul). Then when he ran out to meet him, "he saw as it were the face of God." The healing was immediate.

Learning to "feel" beyond the appearances until we feel the eternal connection with another must precede this oneness experience. Or until we feel the same connection with, say, a flower or an animal. The flower will then thrive, the animal be quiet and subdued. When we see the Life within the criminal, that covering will disappear and the true nature will begin to appear. When we see the Life beyond the condition or disease...that Life will immediately begin to replace the sordid picture. "And mortality will be swallowed up of Life."[17]

With each situation we prove our immediate immortality if we chose to stand in the face of the perverse picture of horror and know who we are. Not with our intellect, our mind, but as the One and only begotten son. Each time we do this and the picture clears and Life appears, we grow closer and closer to our eternal state of being...manifested.

Remember there are two states of consciousness...the Adamic and the Christ. The word Adamic is not speaking of a man named Adam who lived in the garden of God, but of the whole state of humanity in the consciousness of mortality, governed by chance, lawlessness, chaos and confusion. With self-preservation on the throne. So we read, "As in Adam all men die, so in Christ shall all men be made alive."[18] Again, a correction in consciousness, perception is what is needed.

Remember the High Priest went into the most sacred place, which only he could enter, once a year to stand before the heart of Mercy. This would remove the multitudes of coverings and allow the pure and perfect man to appear. He could do this because of Oneness. As he stood there, because there is only One Life, what he prayed and received for one fell upon all. So Jesus became the High Priest for all mankind. As he ascended to the eternal heart of Mercy, he carried his own blood...no longer the blood of an animal. His blood represented the one Life, for the "life is in the blood."[19] Now with the mortal covering removed, we have "no more consciousness of separation (sin)."[20]

Difficult to grasp, I know. But once the reality of this is awakened, it begins to make perfect sense. The entire book of Hebrews is dealing with this. I recommend you begin your study in the Old Testament, with the Tabernacle and the Priesthood. Then go to Hebrews. As you read this over and over, the phenomenal impact of this new dimension will arise in your soul. This is the appearing of the Christ consciousness.

It is not that something real was removed, but our tenacious belief in our inherent unworthiness, guilt and shame...was stripped away. This is the sin consciousness. I call this the Big Lie. This is the only thing truly blocking Oneness from appearing to each one of us. We didn't come with "original sin" and then it was taken away at the cross. What was taken away was a belief only...and that came from religion, man-made religion parroting this throughout the ages. Remember Hebrews, 9:14, tells us that it was the consciousness of sin which was removed.

No! Our true and eternal nature, the very essence of us, made in the image of perfection, ("for you are my masterpiece created in perfection..."}[21] is innocent, mighty and free.

Let's take a look at this idea of the original sin doctrine. This doctrine of men is the reason for all the earth's woes. Either we are formed in the image of our Creator...for "each seed reproduces after its own kind,"[22]...declared by him to be very good...or we came here to suffer for the offence of another. Either we came as the "Light of the world"[23] to swallow up the confusion, or we came to suffer to earn our way back to heaven. In Jeremiah we hear God announce, "Let no more this proverb be spoken in all of Israel...that the fathers have sinned and the children's teeth are set on edge. But rather let each man be responsible for his own offenses."[24]

This insidious doctrine consigns man to a perpetual state of condemnation, unworthiness, guilt and shame. But the "strength of sin is condemnation,"[25] so we are left in a vicious circle of never being able to get off the treadmill of defeat.

This is the veil. This is what was torn away from our hearts at the cross. The entire sin consciousness. The Big Lie. Now, with Daniel, we can boldly declare, "Because innocence was found in me you have shut the mouths of the lions and delivered me."[26]

Where does the "cross" fit in for us now? We are told to "take up our cross daily."[27] Sounds ominous, but it isn't.

Sounds like accepting suffering, but it isn't. I know many "progressive thinkers" scoff at the idea of "the cross," but this is a clear indication that they are living out from intellectualism, rather than Spirit. The cross is simply that we remember daily to choose Life, the One Life. To leave the mortal thinking and reacting behind because we know it has absolutely nothing to do with us. It means to lose any sense of personal possession. We belong to this Life and this Life, all that God is, belongs to us. (Ezekiel 44) So I give over any sense of possessions to him who is the source of it all anyway. I know by doing so he will be able to bless it and when I look again it has increased and is blessed abundantly. This also lets me live without the awful sense of personal responsibility for everything under the sun. I can know "this body, this marriage, this job, these children, all of it, is not mine to worry over. It is all in very good hands now." It leaves me free to be able to hear if there is anything that the Spirit is actually leading me to do about any of it as well. Retaining personal possessions of anything keeps us feeling responsible and blocks us from entering into the Presence of Him to whom all things belong. This would keep us feeling anxious, fearful and totally not trusting. All of which are blocks to Spirit flowing...therefore healing.

If I have suffered an incredible loss and grief is consuming my soul, I have learned to truly give this personal possession, that I thought was mine, over to Him who is the source of it all, and the grief is removed and hope for the increase begins to fill my soul.

At the cross Jesus left behind the mortal identity,

buried it and enjoyed one hundred fold in return, immortal Life! I call this the resurrection principle. You can't lose by giving. Day always follows night. Summer always follows winter. God will fill that space with himself. Just wait and remain in a receptive mode.

We give to God what is his already and in time we receive the increase in return. "While the earth remains, seedtime and harvest, and cold and heat, summer and winter, and day and night shall not cease." (Gen. 8:22) We simply cannot lose when we choose to lose. We simply cannot gain when we choose to cling to whatever. Daily we choose to follow the Lamb wherever he goes, denying the mortal identity in favor of the immortal identity. By doing so we are receiving the grace to live out from that day by day, situation by situation. We choose to wait for the Spirit to lead out in every situation. We trust that it will. By doing this we chose daily to "serve a purpose greater than our own."

This is the true cross experience.

For centuries man has attempted to elevate personal morality as a modality towards true spirituality. But man has failed to achieve this. You will notice an absence of right vs. wrong, good vs. bad as the avenue towards achieving Oneness. The Old Testament strict adherence to the Law is replaced with a much higher path, that of following the Spirit day by day, hour by hour and situation by situation. Gone are the days when we are proud enough to think our "goodness" is a requirement. This duality of thinking cannot enter into this holy space. It causes division, judgment, and arrogance. As we commit ourselves to following the leading of Spirit, "whatsoever things are true, whatsoever things are honest, whatsoever things are just, whatsoever things are pure, whatsoever things are lovely, whatsoever things are of a good report,"[28] will automatically be.

This is the path to the experience of Oneness.

This is the fulfillment of our High and Holy calling.

SCRIPTURE
REFERENCES

CHAPTER ONE

1 Psalm 8:4
2 Matthew 3:8
3 Acts 24: 16
4 Luke 11:2
5 Revelation 21:1
6 Isaiah 11:6
7 Hebrews 8:10-12
   Jeremiah 31:33-34
8 Romans 13:8
9 Psalm 100:3
10 Genesis 1:12
11 1Corinthians 15:53
12 Ephesians 1:4
13 Psalm 90:1-2
14 Philippians 2:5
15 Matthew 11:15
16 Genesis 1:28

17 Luke 17:21
18 Matthew 6:25
19 Matthew 6:10
20 John 12:27
21 Romans 8:19

CHAPTER TWO

1 Matthew 28:18
2 Matthew 28:19
3 Matthew 15:6,14
4 Luke 11:52
5 John 6:28
6 John 16:13-15
7 1John 5:6

CHAPTER THREE

1 John 1:16
2 1Corinthians 13:12
3 Hebrews 4:10
4 Hebrews 4:10
5 John 14:12

CHAPTER FOUR

1 John 5:30
2 Matthew 8:9
   Matthew 21:24
3 Acts 17:28
4 John 3:8
5 John 7:38

CHAPTER FIVE

1 Romans 8:19
2 2Corinthians 5:1
3 Revelation 2:17
   Revelation 22:4
4 Ezekiel 36:26
5 Ephesians 5:30
6 Job 22:21
7 John 17:3
8 2Timothy 2:13

CHAPTER SIX

1 Matthew 9:13
2 James 2:13
3 Genesis 1:27
4 John 10:10
5 Psalm 106:15
6 Isaiah 30:21

CHAPTER SEVEN

1   2 Corinthians 5:19
2   John 1:16
3   1Corinthians 15:28
4   Luke 17:21
5   Ephesians 2:14
6   John 9:4
7   Isaiah 11:9
8   Ephesians 20-22
9   Ephesians 2:6
10 Revelation 21:5

CHAPTER EIGHT

1 Colossians 2:10
2 Hebrews 2:14
3 Matthew 5:36
4 Luke 15

5   Genesis 19

6   Psalm 34:8

7   Matthew 11:29

CHAPTER NINE

1   1Corinthians 15:53

2   Deuteronomy 28:6

3   Revelation 3:12

4   Matthew 6:10

5   1Corinthians 15:28

6   Jeremiah 17:24

7   Genesis 3:24

8   1Samuel 3:19

    Isaiah 55:11

9   Genesis 1:28

10 Micah 4:9

11 Romans 10:6-8

12 Hebrews 5:8

13 Proverbs 25:29

14 Proverbs 29:2

15 Exodus 20:3

16 Ephesians 5:11

17 1Peter 4:17

CHAPTER TEN

1   Ezekiel 44:18

2   John 14:12

3   Hebrews 4:12

4   Ezekiel 44:15

5   Leviticus 17:11

6   Proverbs 16:6

7   Acts 24:16

8   John 20:23

9   Leviticus 16

10 Matthew 9:13

11 James 2:13

12 John 9:39

13 Isaiah 58:6

14 Ephesians 2:10

15 Job 23:14

16 John 16:22

CHAPTER ELEVEN

1   Romans 1:20

2   1Corinthians 15:28

3   Romans 11:36

4   Ephesians 1:10

5   Colossians 1:26

6   1John 4:4

7   Matthew 16:25

8   Isaiah 25:7

9 Isaiah 25:7-8

10 Revelation 21:4-5

11 Ecclesiastes 7:29

12 Matthew 27:51

13 Luke 23:34

14 Job 23:14

15 Isaiah 11:3

16 Genesis 32-33

17 2Corinthians 5:4

18 1Corinthians 15:22

19 Leviticus 17:11

20 Hebrews 9:14

21 Ephesians 2:10

22 Genesis 1:11

23 Matthew 5:14

24 Exekiel 18:2

25 1Corinthians 15:56

26 Daniel 6:22

27 Luke 9:23

28 Philippians 4:8

INTRODUCTION
TO
LIVING BEYOND DISEASE

There are masses of people really searching to understand the true nature of God. They know intuitively that there is a vast difference between, religion's God and the reality of God; between a religious life and a spiritual life.

Equally, there are thousands who are facing health issues of massive proportions, as well as other serious challenges in their lives, and have nowhere to turn for real help.

Living Beyond Disease was brought forth to fill this void. Let me introduce you to some of what we have that will help you. For those of you who may not be familiar with all my books, let me briefly tell you first about them.

Book #1
Of Monkeys and Dragons:
Freedom from the Tyranny of Disease

This was my very first book and I supposed would be my only book. I didn't want to leave this planet, without sharing some of the most extraordinary healings and life-altering experiences I had, the likes of which I never read or heard about anywhere else. These stories and what each one taught me propelled me to where I am today...and where I will be.

This was the "launch book" and is still the most widely sold of the bunch.

Book #2
The God That We've Created:
The Basic Cause of All Disease

This book is based upon the startling discovery that our experiences in life are in direct proportion to our ideas of the nature of God and how God relates to mankind. We find that we accept outrageous difficulties and insurmountable hurdles simply because we believe we're "supposed to." We have found ourselves in total darkness as to the nature of God and his purposes and intentions for man. And the ones who believe they "know" are the ones Jesus spoke of as the "blind leaders of the blind."

Step by step we Biblically challenge endless generations of teachings that have consigned us to the miseries we face. This one is for the humble seekers of truth.

BOOK #3
WHEN THE WOLF IS AT THE DOOR:
THE SIMPLICITY OF HEALING

This is a step by step approach to handling physical difficulties that face us in order to secure the help and healings we seek. This also enables us to realize why we might not be finding what we seek. We find that what we have learned dealing with the physical also applies to any and every situation that can appear to man. Every phase of life responds to these principles.

  * *Reading the first two books first will be a major help in being able to absorb the content in this book.*

BOOK #4
UNSPEAKABLE MERCY:

This might be my favorite simply because the revelation of God as pure Mercy, without any hint of punishment, disappointment, withholding, or judging, made the single greatest impact upon my spiritual existence...and still does. It decimates what we have been taught for generations and gives us the liberty to be free. Free from pain, suffering, loss, lack, all human miseries. God is Love comes off the pages of sermons, songs, and books to explode in Life within the heart.

BOOK #5
ONLY RECEIVE:
NO BARRIERS, NO BOUNDARIES

In our frantic search for the all illusive God we find here that if we would only stop! Stop doing. Stop moving! Stop thinking. Stop crying...long enough to realize that God has been here all along...just waiting for you to receive all he has and all he is. This destroys the idea that some "get it" and some do not. That anything from God must be earned. That we can fail. This points out the reasons why we reach out for what is already here for us and how to cease from this effort. Another major change in my life and understanding.

BOOK #6
JACOB'S LADDER:
PARADISE REGAINED

I have taught on the contents of this book for years. How we progressively come out from the old thinking (and therefore living) to the new and liberating understandings of the true nature of God and what we came here to do...and to be. This is positively the end of playing the role of the human victim in favor of ruling in authority over all evidences of darkness as the true Son(s) of God.

BOOKS #7 - 9
ARISE, SHINE:
VOL. 1, 2 & 3

Each book contains 365 days readings packed with life changing truths gleaned from 15 years of weekly radio shows and 20 years of weekly meetings on Spirituality and Health.

Living Beyond Disease also offers 200 + "teaching" CD's to instruct and encourage those who are facing challenges in their lives, as well as help those who are searching for a deeper understanding of God and what our purpose here truly is.

LIVING BEYOND DISEASE
107 SCENIC LOOP ROAD
BOERNE, TX 78006
(830) 755-8767
WWW.LIVINGBEYONDDISEASE.COM